# Going Places

Aaron Waldeck

Rosen
REAL
READERS

The Rosen Publishing Group, Inc.
New York

1

People go places every day.

Some people ride bikes.

Some people ride in a car.

Some people ride on a bus.

Some people ride on a plane.

Some people like to walk!

# Words to Know

bikes

bus

car

plane